About (the) Illustrator

Name: ....

Age: .... Hometown: ....

One great thing about my Grandpa is:

....

....

One of the best days we spent together was when:

....

....

If I were magical, I'd be able to:

....

....

Grandpa is Magical

COMPENDIUM®

kids™

inspiring possibilities.™

This is my Grandpa.

You can tell he's magical.

When he pours a glass of milk, the milk turns into a rainbow of colors.

"How do you do that?"
I ask him. He says he's
not allowed to say.

It's hard to play hide-and-seek with him because he can disappear.

He makes his feet disappear first and then keeps going.

"Watch this," Grandpa says, as he makes a crazy creature appear from thin air.

Then the creature performs an amazing trick just for me. *✳* *✳*

Grandpa and I decide to make a fort out of things we have around the house.

It's huge!

I discover something
wonderful inside.

When the day is ending, Grandpa finds a way to push the sun back up into the sky.

"There's still so much more to do today!" he says.

After dinner, Grandpa creates a cloud that rains delicious candies over the table.

Some of them have a surprise inside when I open the wrapper.

Then it's time for bed. Grandpa pulls a star from the sky for me and puts it on my pillow.

"Sleep tight," he says, "tomorrow is going to be another magical day."

WITH SPECIAL THANKS TO THE
ENTIRE COMPENDIUM FAMILY.

CREDITS:

Written by: M.H. Clark
Designed by: Julie Flahiff
Edited by: Amelia Riedler

ISBN: 978-1-938298-33-2

1st printing. Printed in China with soy inks. A011404001

COMPENDIUM®

kids

inspiring possibilities.™